Copyright © 202

All rights reserved

The characters and events portrayed in this book are fictitious. Any similarity to real persons, living or dead, is coincidental and not intended by the author.

No part of this book may be reproduced, or stored in a retrieval system, or transmitted in any form or by any means, electronic, mechanical, photocopying, recording, or otherwise, without express written permission of the publisher.

Cover design by: Leonardo.A.i.
Copyright: 9798339014751

Printed in the United States of America

To the families and children who treasure their "silly gadgets"—our phones, tablets, and screens—this book is for you. In a world where it's easy to get lost in pixels and buttons, let's not forget what matters most: the laughter, stories, and connections we share with each other. Look around, appreciate the beauty in your surroundings, the warmth of a smile, the love of those close by, and yes, even the goldfish who's been waiting very patiently for his dinner! Here's to finding balance, cherishing life, and making space for the moments that truly matter.

"The more time you spend with your nose in a screen, the more you're missing the world right in front of you... like a fish begging for dinner or a dog chewing your shoes."

FRANKY- THE LOYAL, LOVABLE, AND VERY HUNGRY- GOLDFISH

PREFACE

Before we dive into the chaos of missing cellphones, rampaging puppies, and one *very* hungry fish, let's just take a moment to appreciate how much we all love our "silly boxes"- those magical screens that seem to control our lives. But what happens when the screens take over, and no one notices the world around them anymore? Well, that's exactly what happens in this story. You'll meet Franky, the fish with a lot to say, and a family who's about to learn that sometimes, you've just got to look up and see the world- including the dog chewing your game controller! So, get ready for a wild adventure and remember: it's not just about the screens; it's about everything (and everyone) around them.

Now, let's find out what happens when the *real* action begins- without Wi-Fi.

THE DOG ATE MY CELLPHONE!

Kaitlyn Marie Garza

"Hello! H e l l o ! Anyone home!? I'm starving over here!" Franky the fish pleaded. "I need fooood" he yelled even louder.

THE DOG ATE MY CELLPHONE!

"Sheesh, tough crowd," Franky mumbled, swishing his tail. "Do I need to sing "Under the Sea" to get some love around here? I mean, I'm practically related to Sebastian!"

if fourteenth cousin twice removed counts...

THE DOG ATE MY CELLPHONE!

Papa, Mama, Child One, and Child Two were...a bit distracted.

Papa was glued to the big magic square. **Click-click-click**, and the screen flashed and beeped. Every time the screen flashed, Papa acted like he'd just discovered buried treasure, but **nope,** just another cat video.

THE DOG ATE MY CELLPHONE!

Mama was talking to herself again with a black rectangle attached to her head. She walked around the house, waving her arms like she was trying to swat invisible flies. No one seemed to notice her strange behavior...

weird.

THE DOG ATE MY CELLPHONE!

Child One and Child Two were bouncing around like two squirrels on sugar clutching the weirdest contraption ever- an odd machine with buttons, dials, and probably a few rocket launchers (who knows?!).

THE DOG ATE MY CELLPHONE!

Their fingers flew across it so fast, it looked like they were playing hot potato with a volcano. Every now and then, they'd leap into the air like popcorn, or freeze, staring at the screen with such intensity you'd think it was a math test.

Honestly, it was hard to tell.

THE DOG ATE MY CELLPHONE!

"But does anyone pay attention to hungry, lonely Franky?" he grumbled. "NOPE. They don't even notice that Child One's pants are on backwards!"

THE DOG ATE MY CELLPHONE!

Then, suddenly, "Aha! I have a brilliant idea!"
Franky said, his fins fluttering with excitement.
He grabbed his trusty seashell and called his buddy Carl.

"CARL! Help! I'm starving! These humans are way too distracted by their silly gadgets.

THE DOG ATE MY CELLPHONE!

"Ah. Yes... I've seen this before," Carl said. "Classic case of C.E.F. — Chronic Electronic Fever."

THE DOG ATE MY CELLPHONE!

"Oooh, that sounds bad!" gasped Franky.

THE DOG ATE MY CELLPHONE!

"Indeed, it is. But, there is a cure... but it might get...

messy" Carl said with a grin in his voice.

THE DOG ATE MY CELLPHONE!

"Messy? I like messy," Franky grinned back.

THE DOG ATE MY CELLPHONE!

A few days later, there was a knock—err—woof... at the door. "WOOF! WOOF!"

THE DOG ATE MY CELLPHONE!

Papa opened it. His jaw dropped.

"Whoa! It's the pup-arazzi!"

THE DOG ATE MY CELLPHONE!

Hundreds of dogs covered the front lawn,

barking and wagging their tails.

THE DOG ATE MY CELLPHONE!

Before Papa could react, the door burst open, and the frenzy began.

THE DOG ATE MY CELLPHONE!

The pups tumbled in like a furry tidal wave, skidding across the floor, knocking over lamps, and bouncing off furniture.

THE DOG ATE MY CELLPHONE!

"NOOOO!" Papa, Mama, Child One, and Child Two screamed in unison.

Chaos erupted.

THE DOG ATE MY CELLPHONE!

One puppy grabbed a slipper and raced around the room, turning the living room into a racetrack.

Made in the USA
Las Vegas, NV
07 October 2024

96420038R00017

LOGUE:
pent's Whisper

y that if you

ely on quiet nights

ea, you can still

aga King's

n the waves—a

hat the bond

eang Neak and

ng, between the

d the prince,

to guide the land

ia, its people, and

blessings of the
 ir children will
 their legacy,
 inding the land
 ea, the past and
 e, in an
 ble bond.

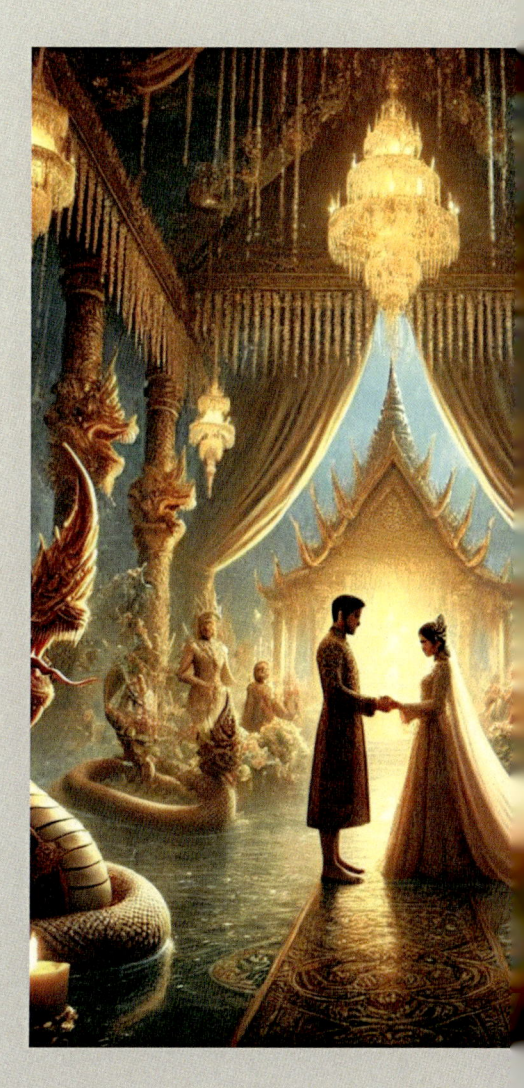

PTER 6:

Ceremony of Legacy

nor, the kingdom

the "Serpent Bond"

a tradition that will

down through

s. To this day, the

eah Thong and

k is celebrated in

dings, where the

s the bride's scarf

l of protection and

e, much like the

mbrace.

The union of the h[ ]
prince and the ser[ ]
princess symboliz[es]
eternal connection[ ]
the earth and the [ ]
physical and the [ ]
and most importa[nt]
union of two cultu[res]
Indian and Khmer[ ]
love forms the be[ ]
upon which a futu[re]
will rise.

CHAPTE

Founding the Kingdo

Returning to the la

Thong and **Neang N**

crowned as the firs

of Funan, a kingdor

blends the ancient

of the Naga with th

knowledge and pow

distant lands. Toge

lay the foundation

empire that will on

grow into the migh

civilization.

nion is blessed,
ak gifts him a
eapon-a golden
ed from serpent
mbolizing the
 of the Naga
. In exchange,
ng vows to lead
om, ensuring the
dom's legacy will
gh their

PTER 4:

om Beneath the Sea

ir bond, Neang

Preah Thong to her

gdom beneath the

Preah Thong

he splendor of the

zation-a world

 by glowing corals,

s of gold rising

ean floor. He learns

of the land and sea,

d power, of the

 connection to

 future.

Through wit, bravery

unshakeable love for

Neak, Preah Thong

odds, completing the

earning the **Naga Ki**

...tic action sequence
...s **Preah Thong** uses
...ls, determination,
...ivine strength to
...me the relentless
... elemental attacks.

...rms, tidal waves,
...akes, and violent
...nverge on him, but
... remains unshaken.

Preah Thong uses hi
strength to navigate
battling spectral w
evading traps, and c
the tormented soul

The action build
uncovers secrets
Neang Neak's past
that their union h
prophesied for ce

ong must brave the
cean on a mystical
boat,

g off massive sea

s he searches for the

otus in the darkest

depths.

To prove his wort[h,]
Thong is set three
impossible tasks: [find a]
rare flower that b[looms]
only once in a tho[usand]
years, survive the
bite of a serpent [god,]
and venture into t[he]
depths of the oce[an to]
retrieve a sacred [item]
guarded by monst[rous]
creatures.

CHAPTE

The Serpent Ki

Before they can uni **Thong** must face th challenge: gaining approval of the **Na** The serpent deity r the ocean, his mass coiling around the storm. He is not ea swayed, for no hum ever been permitte the Naga bloodline

nt their eyes

e stands still. But

is not without

s. **Neang Neak's**

ound by ancient

ans are forbidden

Naga realm. The

ngdom, hidden

ne ocean's depths,

ets that are not

mortal eyes.

CHAPTE

The Enchante
and the Serpent

One evening, as the m

ripples over a hidden

Thong stumbles upon

mesmerizing sight. Da

the water's edge is **N**

daughter of the **Naga**

beauty is unlike anyth

ever seen-her long, da

flows like a river, her

with the magic of the

bloodline. Unbeknow

she is more than just

she is a guardian of t

sacred waters.

His journey is peri

marked by raging s

and treacherous wa

But his path chang

night when his shi

crashes into the sh

mysterious and un

land-Cambodia. He

jungles hum with

the earth pulses w

ancient power, and

horizon is filled w

untold possibilitie

...PTER 1:
...xiled Prince

...shimmering
...f Cambodia, in the
...rts of India, **Prince**
...lives a life of
...naware that destiny
...plans. But after a
...val in his royal
...oung prince is
...ed to leave behind
...e knows. Armed
...g but his courage and
...s into the unknown,
...r redemption and a
...ng.

...LOGUE:

...y of the Serpent King

...ep, mystical waters
...ent seas, the **Naga**
...s-a powerful serpent
...protects the land
...ple. One fateful
...ophecy emerges
...ars: a prince from a
...d will unite with
...er, **Neang Neak**, to
...dom destined to
...uture of a great

THE DOG ATE MY CELLPHONE!

Another puppy jumped onto the kitchen counter, sending dishes crashing to the floor with a loud clatter. CRASH!

THE DOG ATE MY CELLPHONE!

Another pup chomped on Child One and Child Two's box with finger rocket launchers wagging his tail happily.

THE DOG ATE MY CELLPHONE!

Meanwhile, two others played tug-of-war with Mama's favorite pillow...

THE DOG ATE MY CELLPHONE!

"**Stop them!**" Mama shrieked as a puppy rolled headfirst into a potted plant, sending soil flying everywhere.

THE DOG ATE MY CELLPHONE!

Meanwhile, another pup tried to climb the curtains, its little paws slipping, creating a chaotic swing that pulled down the curtain rod.

THE DOG ATE MY CELLPHONE!

Child One and Child Two tried to chase the puppies but only ended up tripping over them, landing in a giggling heap as more puppies zoomed around them like little furry tornadoes.

THE DOG ATE MY CELLPHONE!

R.I.S.G.P. — Rest in Silly Gadgets Peace.

All the gadgets and gizmos were lost

in the puppy stampede.

THE DOG ATE MY CELLPHONE!

"Yikes! That's gonna leave a mark," Franky whispered from his tank. "But maybe now I'll get some food!" he said with a wink.

A few days later...

Without a single gadget in sight, no buzzing phones, no flashing tablets, and no "just one more cat video," Papa, Mama, Child One, Child Two, and Franky (the ever-patient, ever-hungry fish) spent time together, laughing so hard their bellies ached.

THE DOG ATE MY CELLPHONE!

They couldn't stop giggling about the *Great Puppy Invasion*.

"Remember when that one puppy tried to swing from the curtains and ended up with a lampshade on his head?" Papa chuckled, wiping a tear from his eye.

THE DOG ATE MY CELLPHONE!

"And YOU tried to chase him while holding Franky's fishbowl like a football!" Mama laughed.

Franky swam in a circle, giving a big fishy sigh. "Ah, yes. My hero. Next time, leave the rescue mission to the pros."

THE DOG ATE MY CELLPHONE!

The family hadn't realized how much fun a little chaos could bring. Sure, their gadgets became a mountain of **slobbery** chew toys, and yeah, the house still smelled faintly of wet dog, but they wouldn't trade it for the world.

THE DOG ATE MY CELLPHONE!

Child One and Child Two giggled. "Maybe next time we'll have a chicken stampede!"

"Let's not push our luck," Franky mumbled. "I *barely* survived the puppies!"

THE DOG ATE MY CELLPHONE!

"*Finally,* Franky thought, *the family understood that even in the craziest moments, there was something special. It wasn't in their screens or gadgets, but in the laughter, the stories, and the amazing feeling of being* together *as a family.*"

THE DOG ATE MY CELLPHONE!

Franky swam to the top of his tank, gave his most charming fishy wink, and said, "Now, can we **please** *embrace* the chaos of **FEEDING ME DINNER**?"

THE DOG ATE MY CELLPHONE!

KAITLYNMARIEGARZA

The End

THE DOG ATE MY CELLPHONE!

ABOUT THE AUTHOR

Kaitlyn Marie Garza

When Kaitlyn isn't busy dreaming up stories, she's probably out exploring the great outdoors with her family, two mischievous dogs, and a cat that's convinced it's the boss.

As a proud mom, a pediatric occupational therapist, and a psychology student, Kaitlyn understands the power of imagination and laughter. She's on a mission to give kids everywhere stories that make them smile, giggle, and maybe even press pause on their tablets! GASP!

Kaitlyn lives in a magical world where anything is possible—especially if it involves family and a goofy laugh. She's the author of multiple children's stories, and when she's not writing, you can find her building forts, climbing mountains (okay, maybe just small hills), or perfecting her dance moves (spoiler alert: they're hilarious).

BOOKS BY THIS AUTHOR

Willa The Wolf's Courageous Adventure

Kit The Kangaroo's Tail: A Story Celebrating Differences

Andy The Anteater And The Ants In His Pants

Gabby's Great Big Emotional Faint-Outs: A Faint-Tastical Story Of Feelings

THE DOG ATE MY CELLPHONE!

Made in the USA
Las Vegas, NV
07 October 2024